The Rose of Toulouse

FRED D'AGUIAR was born in London in 1960 of Guyanese parents and grew up in Guyana. He returned to London for his secondary education and trained as a psychiatric nurse at the Maudsley Hospital in London before studying at the University of Kent for his BA in English with African and Caribbean Studies. He has published six volumes of poetry and five novels. He lives in the USA and teaches at Virginia Tech.

T0096382

Also by Fred D'Aguiar from Carcanet Press

Continental Shelf

FRED D'AGUIAR

The Rose of Toulouse

CARCANET

First published in Great Britain in 2013 by
Carcanet Press Limited
Alliance House
Cross Street
Manchester M2 7AQ

www.carcanet.co.uk

A CIP catalogue record for this book is available from the British Library

ISBN 978 1 84777 229 9

The publisher acknowledges financial assistance from Arts Council England

Typeset by XL Publishing Services, Exmouth
Printed and bound in England by SRP Ltd, Exeter

For Dylan

Acknowledgements

Some of these poems first appeared in the following publications: *American Scholar, Best British Poetry 2011, Dublin Poetry Review* (online at http://www.dublinpoetryreview.ie/), *Edinburgh Review, Fulcrum 3, The Guardian, Island, Poetry London, Poetry Review, The Times Literary Supplement, Red, The Same, Small Axe Salon, The Wolf.* Other poems were commissioned for and published in the anthologies *A Room To Live In* (ed. Tamar Yoseloff), *New Writing 12, The Ropes* (ed. Sophie Hannah and John Hegley), and *Velocity* (ed. Maja Priusnitz). Some of the poems have been broadcast on *The Verb*, BBC Radio 4. 'Dalí on Dickens' was a commission for *A Mutual Friend: Poems for Charles Dickens* edited by Peter Robinson, introduced by Adrian Poole (Two Rivers Press & The English Association). 'Legal Tender' was commissioned by Arts Council England for its celebration of the 200th anniversary of the abolition of slavery and webcast on the ACE website. 'Emily Dickinson: How Does Your Garden Grow?', which appears here in revised form, began life as a commission to commemorate BBC Radio 3's re-broadcast in November 2010 of Aaron Copland's arrangement of eight poems by Emily Dickinson, produced by Julian May. 'The Giant of Land's End' was published in the Aark chapbook series edited by Sudeep Sen.

Contents

Politics

Today's sun looks nothing like yesterday's
Great ball of fire – goodness, gracious – that plummeted
Behind Brush Mountain in Blacksburg, Virginia.

Today's sun holds a steady white flame to stubborn fog
Grazing willy-nilly among trees, hills, valleys.

Rigged

Here comes a fisherman with a lead-fringed net
He gathers, swings and throws in a circle

At the sky above water and the circle falls,
Joins its pleated reflection,
BP spill folding back into itself in reverse,
All slick and no glitter in that fisherman's catch.

Key West

Dawn begins in my skull,
flits from right to left,
back to front, searching
for an exit. I open my eyes.

Dawn builds a bedroom
instantly to house itself,
walls that absorb light,
a ceiling light drips from,

floors with creases
full of trapped dirt
only light squeezes
sideways through.

I cross to my bedroom window,
each muscle, every stretch
and contraction a point of light.
The points expand and join,

making this body of bright bones,
translucent flesh and blood
for battery-acid; this engine.
Single piston and cylinders.

I open those blinds.
Let light build a world
barely able to contain itself;
itself barely contained.

Excise

Each year I travel, my passport photo
looks less like me. Two of us
trick our way through customs.

My heart dances and I tell myself,
Don't breathe so shallow,
when I face a uniform block

my path, unlike my laminated
photo tucked in my breast pocket,
locked in amber and oblivious.

I age for both of us at double speed.
My silent partner keeps his poker face,
I do the talking for the two of us.

Nights, I dream this face but not my life,
leaving me with a sour taste and smell,
longing for a country not on any map:

to be the man who crosses borders
without a passport; whose face matches
curved lines that spell my name.

The official behind Plexiglass
takes her time, looks me up and down.
I speak as she scans my passport

and watches for what the screen brings
up about me. I've no idea what she sees
that makes her ask about my line of work.

I answer with a face
that's stranger to my passport every day,
telling lies about a life not lived, not his.

Boy Soldier

What a smile! One large lamp for a face,
smaller lanterns where skin stretches over
bones waiting for muscle, body all angles.

His Kalashnikov fires at each moving
thing before he knows what he drags
down. He halts movement of every
kind and fails to weigh whom he stops

dead or maims, his bullets
like jabs thrown before the thought
to throw them, involuntary shudders
when someone, somewhere, steps over

his shallow, unmarked, mass grave.
But his smile remains undimmed,
inviting, not knowing what hit him,
what snuffs out the wicks in his eyes.

Except that he moves and a face just like
his figures like him to stop all action
with a flick of finger on the trigger.

War on Terror

Lasts for as long as nightmares

paint behind the eyelids

long as a measure of cord

cut from a navel remains buried

under a tamarind tree

not long after the eyes wash away

last night's paint

no longer than a piece of string

tied at a navel

Wartime Aubade

I hear them before I see them
Their song as though music might run out

Rapid twitters mingle with lazy burbles
Instruments warm up in pattern and rhythm

Light answers a summons from the east
Pushing aside this thick and heavy curtain

The day's first truck crests Brush Mountain
Dragging a parachute of engine noise

Stop me before I run away with myself
To join an army of beaks and feathers

A light brigade pouring over the horizon
A dark enemy driven into the eaves

Trace

There's no love lost
Between the time kept by hills
And the smell left by an animal
Just out of sight and
No worse loss than that love

9 am on this hill of hills
Spreads sunlight with a trowel
Shaped by overnight dew
Speckled with hoof, claw and foot
Prints and my thumb
Thrown in for good measure

There's no lost love
Between the hills kept by time
And the animal left by a smell
So strong that it waters sight
No worse love than that loss

The hills dynamited for fuel
Their tops cut off like scalps
The rivers panned for doing nothing
Sunflowers grow tired marking time
Kept by forests with a sell-by date

There's no loss, love,
Between the kept hills of time
And the animal smell left
Out just for sight and
No loss worse than love

Monday Morning

where water drops
rock-face chatters

bone flesh-covered
between teeth tongue

tied for want of air
sucked from bedrooms

ruled by cubicles
painted ochre by hands

manicured overnight
under angled lamplight

where bones crush
ground to dust

skin flies off face
peeled by whip

bullet and bomb
radars guide and index

fingers launch from
cumulo-cirrus

water sky basket leak
flood drowns rock

Shoes My Father Wore

I write in my head to keep my head right.
50 dawns on me and opens my mouth.

Mouth jumps off my face and asks me
where I want it to go next.

On my feet I say but look down
dumb and see only my father's feet

where mine should be and his shoes
flirting with my fallen mouth.

So I sign, badly, with some urgency,
before time runs out, speak fast,

speak loud as the day looks long,
my dear, bared soles.

His shoes on my feet becomes my shoes
on his feet. My feet take on his,

transplanted on my body,
his heels click and I dance.

The Lady with the Purple Glove

I'm sorry I'm going to have to stick you again,
Says the one my mother always complained about,

The phlebotomist whose hair matches
Her gloves, whose latex smells of burning flesh.

She wears a Joker's mask and purple specs.
She draws blood like a noodle pulled from

My arm by way of my nose, throat and ear.
She fills two glass ampoules deep as vats,

Tall as silos, and it is her sharp incisors
I see last when my head tailspins.

Underwater

Sky seems round each time she cries
Trees knit fingers and thumbs over the road
Providing complete cover from sky fruit
Straight road longer than sight

Girl in her keeps looking over shoulder
Woman tells her this only wastes time
Look how flat sky curves when you cry
Glance back for another on the road

Her bare feet pick up splinters she ignores
For now but must fish out with a needle later
This sky cradles the night and gestates the day
This road measures her years end to end

A woman ruled by a fifteen-year-old girl
A road fenced by trees full of sky

Wednesday's Child

I wake to birds I cannot see, singing in the trees.
Birds make me think – trees sing. A sun, in stripes,
Shimmies across my bedroom,

Between bed, dresser and door, poised to slip on
My bedroom slippers, and run my day, disguised as me,
My best and brightest side.

I drive to work in a mood that eases my right foot
Off the accelerator, and look out all sides of the car.
One season is besting another in the New Valley,

I sit in my office and power up my university computer
For my routine: scan email and open a blank page
Ready for my conjuring trick.

Your message, son, first thing, catches my eye.
You confirm your diagnosis of MS, by Britain's experts,
Who triple-check, then call what they see.

And there I am, nothing, if not a feather, freed from a bird
Shaking dew off its wings, barely something, I float
And fall, out of time, in slow motion,

Back to you riding your first bike, with me running
Beside you, one hand ready to grab the seat in case
You tilt too far, doing my best to keep up,

Until you speed up, leave me behind, and you whoop
At your magic stay upright, in a fluid, straight line
That opens yards between us.

Son, keep your songs on the tip of your tongue,
For your balance on the beam of this morning's sun,
For your gravity-defying float down,

A feather, sunlight in your hair, the flute of that bird,
Your hands steering the wheel of your bike,
Your feet kicking and pedals' whirr.

Yesterday's News

My son is in heavy disguise,
The fisheries won't let him weigh
His scales, just three, one blue, one
Yellow, one green.
                    He wears a helmet
Over his helmet and a coat beneath
His shirt, and says, with his usual
Bristling conviction:
                        I'm absolutely fine dad
nothing has changed for me,
I will definitely email you
When I find out more.
You and mum shouldn't worry (sic)
This is nothing.
                      It is something. Son,
You lie on an altar of bones and teeth, a knife
Scrapes your fine hairs and scales –
Not the principal beauty à la Bishop
But damn near as much –
Off your toned body.
                    I grab the hand
That wields the blade, and throw my
Chest in front of yours, in the line
Of that knife-thrust.
                    Stay behind me,
Son, just this once, do not work your way
Back to the front of me, I do this
Not for you but for myself.

The Dream Giver

Who offers me keys to a car, fitted out
For you, and your new incarnation as a beetle?

The dream I squint at to see, and cup my hands
Around my ear to catch, speeds away,

Leaving just us two, and what looks like
A family camper with a hospital bed,

That telltale metal rail to keep you from
Rolling onto the floor – no discernible hospital

Corners, no bleach smell, nor ultra-white
Strip lights, but the giver keeps a coiffed head

Steady, as she recedes from my protest.
This leaves just you, me, and a set of keys

You look at and beckon for with a nod, that I hand
Over, all dropped jaws, dry mouth and wide eyes.

You wave me off and begin your gangly climb
Into your nest, your huff, puff and teeter-totter.

So this dream empties of you, leaving me;
My owl's 360° search for something to latch on to.

Letter from King Ferdinand of Spain to the Tainos
in October 1493

My wife waits for me
in our unmade bed. She bruises
easily against my bones.
We fit together when I see fit.
She leaves me with an ache
not there when I approach her
nameless, no date in mind,
my bones fitted to a spine curved
by time, time and again by a ring,
ring and ding dong.

Icy bones in my bony bed,
not mine alone, more yours
than mine. Bones scrambled,
hieroglyphics lost to me now
in my coupling with history, curled
here beside me in a fitful sleep
typical of a body without blame,
yet one full of dreams. You see,
or refuse to see, that history,
with a hey and a ho and lo,

is my mistress. I am in a bed
made for bones sweetened
with milk and rice, milk turned
by time, a grain of rice for each
turn, each time we turn, each second
we share. History with nothing
lying beside it but my still bones
pared of flesh, bones unshackled,
bones that mark time, porous time,
and more of the same
in the same old, same old.

Legal Tender

1.
I wait so long
I stand so still
Swallows sit on my
Shoulders and wash
In the fonts at my neck
I carry rain
Two cups' worth
In the dippers of my
Clavicles
I have no energy
To shoo them
One pecks something
From the stubble on my
Priced and purchased chin
I look old before my
Time while my time
Makes me look
Older than I should be
Both are not the same
One is a set of lines
Chiselled in my forehead
The other curlicues
My spine and spirit
Spirit is the negative
In this picture of me
What I store in the crook
Of my arms where
The natural light
Plunges into darkness
I send from my time
To yours
I want to blink
I wish to roll my shoulders
Stretch my arms
Empty my clavicles
Of what's pooled there

More than a pulse
In my neck
Less than a breath
Touch my dry eyes
With your fingers
Dipped in free rain

2.
Old man's head
Grafted to young
Underfed body

All skin and sharp
Bones and not
Much gristle

Polished skin
Refracts light
Sinews harbour

Shadows that
Define how this
Freed slave owns

Less than his
Owner's name
How his body

Looks as if
An increase
In daylight

Might make us see
Not this man
In this light

Not a freed slave
But the heads
Of our parents

Planted on the
Round shoulders
Of our children

3.
As ordered
I wash with soap
History's soap

Hot on my skin
Onion skin
Crackles off me

I wash off layers
Of black for what's
White underneath

Then raw red
Till I shine
Tin-whistle-clean

Play something

Dreamboat

A ship sailed
through my body:
my ribs for rigging,
my lungs for sails,
my backbone
for a main mast.
All my cargo
were children
of the Middle
Passage, bound
for slavery, or an
unceremonious
burial at sea –
all this in my one
landlocked body.

I tried to steer
the ship back
to the slave coast
by sheer will,
my skull for a bridge,
my hands lashed
to the wheel,
my eyes a crow's nest
searching for Africa.

My legs kicked,
my arms pulled,
my lungs filled.
I was food for fish.
I sank in clouded deep.
The ship sailed on.

Wish

I wish those tall ships at Africa's shore
Had dropped anchor to plant crops there:
Sugarcane, tobacco, cotton and coffee.

Instead they filled the hungry bellies
Of hulls with Africans and set sail
Wanting nothing from that big place

That wasn't diamond, gold, ivory, flesh.
I wind the clocks back and turn the ships
Around, not a single bullet, whip, or cutlass

Sound to deafen our ears for centuries.
No Atlantic road of bones from people
Dumped into the sea to form a wake.

News from Nowhere

The sea handles laundry
with the ambition of an illegal
washed to the wrong promontory,

one where the masters fly
outdated flags, drink too early,
and brag about the old gal,

then fancy the maid, call her
Mary, who tries hard not to draw
attention to her nimble footprint,

who wants nothing more
than to wrap the last wave,
reduce those flaps and ease the rent

on her aching bones. The sea stabs
her, scores lines on her skin.
Mary's hospital corners prove

unruly as shorelines and unfold.
Sshh the boss urges. He grabs
Mary, rolls her onto her back,

and she loses herself in waves
that scrub until they erase stacks
of reasons to leave, and excuses

why she cannot listen to news
about a three-card trick of a hand
dealt to her by the sea, knowing what

she ran from held more than
this promise of trouble with laundry,
this sea's rank spray, and fury.

English

My tongue licks clean for salt,
my nose burrows into for other
mineral traces, tired of inhaling dust.
Look with your eyes, a voice tells me,
not those in your head that look out.
I see ice floes, pulled apart by a current.
Salt strafes the air, cracks my lips.
I flow in a westerly direction tugged
by water. I tear through mist, a web,
muslin, skin, or each lets me in.
I look into and delve inside a mirror.
I hear scratching and a spring, my lips
pop into a microphone, my tongue
clacks on my mineral-coated palate.

'English,' the children call
following so close I could reach out,
take one child on each spread finger,
'English.' I should never ask
directions to my childhood,
land the Atlantic tilts towards
threatening to empty into the capital,
send a tidal wave to the whitewashed
house and ripening paddy fields
in country where I ran barefoot,
shirt tail flying and a hole in my crotch
my penis sometimes found its way
through and the girls shrieked at
in amusement and amazement.

In the other capital where English
fits me, tailor-made, I am told to go
back home. But they call me English
there, I protest. Somewhere
midway over the Atlantic, America,
England and Guyana blend in cloud,
sun, air and rain. They join seamlessly,

or mix without evidence of a join.
That's me sorted in shapes made
by clouds, me flying without benefit
of wings or a passport, moving freely
between places and no name strong
enough to stick to my skin, except sea,
sun, air, and the minerals in all three.

Life

When we placed the vase by her bed and she
Inclined her head towards it, a sphere for a sun
Ducked clear of clouds and bathed her in goodness

Knows what. When a breeze caught the bouquet
It filled the room and the rest of the house
With the tang of summer and there was no way

Anything but life could stand that room and us
In it with this shared will to carry on powered
By a sun in each flower and those flowers

With us as their followers towards more light.

Dalí on Dickens

Years from now, measured by a Dalí clock,
Worn on a bony wrist, in a Dickens morality tale,

You turn to me, on our rhetorical armchair, traded
For that chaise longue, when to say French fry

Constituted an infraction, or a senate motion
Up for heated talk on the floor, you take my

Pale hand, hold on for dear life and blurt out
In one breath, as if all the air upped and left:

We waited too long for this to mean anything.
We squandered time as if granted infinite lives.

We forgot all about love, the one thing worth
Something in a life of little or no value, if

The armies on standby mean what they say.
None of our actions while apart fed our love.

Now we are too old to get up from that sofa.
We look at each other and see regret on a skeleton.

Time melts from the fine bones at wrist and ankle,
The seconds ping and ping into a metal bucket,

Planted between us for catching time on the run
To a more worthwhile place with us not there.

Calvino

What did you mean by eponymous,
When you described that city on the hill
Modelled after a cloudscape, adrift,
Whose architects wore togas and crowns?

I've worn away the heels of countless
Practical shoes trying to find out,
My head tipped to receive the right signal,
Eyes glued to my feet, arms ready to break

My fall, steps without footfall, not gingerly,
With my inner ear cooking up the interior
Of a conch shell I need two hands to steady
As I pour its air into mine, so gravity whispers,

Much like turning a sock inside out and feeding
My foot into it so that it ends up around my foot
Right side out, no room left for air, fabric
For skin I can peel off and change at will;

Nothing like seeing the city from high up
Through a wine glass that turns the whole place
Upside down and miniaturised to grace
A nimble wrist, not dainty, too many veins,

Not dipped in any pond, and certainly not pale,
A wrist that invites my lips to the point
Where a butterfly appears trapped under skin,
Stretched, fragrant, almost translucent.

In Memoriam

George in Georgetown, Guyana,
Aged ninety and no longer counting.
Out early mornings and early evenings,
Blocked off entire hours from
12 to 4 for rest in his air-conditioned
Pad, and who could blame him?
Noon bakes bitumen soft
As a cookie pulled from an oven.

Some say Guyanese wood yields
To the artist's chisel twice:
First thing in the morning,
And last thing at night;
In between the two the blade
May break or the wood spoil
Any shape an artist tries to coax
From it no matter how gentle
The tap, tap, tap, for wine,
Gum, milk, for the next line.

George was born in Georgetown,
City made of wood, whose famous,
Large, wooden cathedral keeps
Cool all day, just as wood shields
Any shape, there for the asking,
In the language chisels speak,
But never in the middle of the day;
George knew this as the Guyanese way.

Love

left me stirred, high and dry,
high in the alps of my senses,

dry as salt fish I reconstitute
for a stew of salt fish choker
and a brew at the mercy of her

touch and stone stare, lick and
polish, or should that be Polish,
for that unexplored back of my hand.

Break out the dominoes,
crack open that bottle of rum;
we take turns to slap our hand

on a tin table bar into the small hours;
we lean on each other and stagger home
on a song even the strays find grating;

at least one of us wakes up on the wrong
side of the bed, at least one comes to
his senses in the wrong head and bed.

19 Victoria Street, Shrewsbury

for Geoff Hardy and Peter Roscoe

In this attic overlooking
March mirrored in a river,
Shrewsbury's colonial column,
Almost one mile away, beckons.
A spotlighted Lord Hill, hoisted
Two hundred yards nearer
Posterity, among church steeples
Sprinkled by a fair spread of faithful,
Football stadium floodlights,
And flocks in half a mind to migrate.
I wish a face on this Lord and less
Blood than his credentials
Advertise. I wish him back
Down to earth for history's sake.

Daybreak strengthens Lord Hill's
Plinth and outline and weakens
My resolve to reform his past.
Cars gear up, a train pulls away
From Shrewsbury and more birds
Land on the river, or circle the house
Than I can count. Blame today's
Enabling light for all this industry,
For all that is wrong with civilisation!
Light shows the way for good or ill.
In this particular dawn even the gentry
Soften into a shadow of concrete,
Even water reveals its skin,
No more than a sheen wiped away

By breeze, skin that covers
Onion layers, there as hard light,
Light that paints the frosted air
Crimson. I think the river is black
Because of this skin, a black giant,
Reclined across this town. Just then
Four mallards lift off as one, push from

Water, their feathers prune the air,
They swerve up taking the river's skin
With them, peeling off skin to leave water
Raceless again, like light and mist,
So that Lord Hill towering over
Black water conquers an element
Rather than black people.

And the only race is river current
Winding down to the weir,
One last bridge to limbo under,
Another town ahead for it to divide,
Pacify with kind reflections,
If only because those four mallards
Will soon rest on Lord Hill's effigy,
Make their statue-honouring birdcalls
Then touch down again with those Vs –
Trails that widen on water and spread
A bird's legs to reveal, not a scar,
Opening, or any protuberance,
Just the planed, smooth face
Water turns towards light,

Smooth features, wrinkled by a breeze,
Unwrinkled by calm, that contain a sky.
Water with such a soft touch that it keeps
Dry a loose feather sliding on glass
Hardened in light to an iron mask,
So that everything seen in this light, all
Shrewsbury's steeples, football
Stadium, fields, cellphone towers
And solitary, promoted aristocrat
Isolated on his island paradise
In the middle of a roundabout, all
Remain captive and captivating,
Historyless as night, beautiful as black
Skinned water, and true in this first light.

Lord Hill (1772–1828), Member of Parliament for Shrewsbury in 1812, distinguished
himself at the battle of Waterloo. He became Wellington's second in command,
then General Commander-in-Chief of the British Army.

A Concrete Walk in the Woods

1.
Did we skip careful not to trip
over cracks on paving stones?
Was there a song to match each
hop, step and jump along an entire
block, from corner to corner
stone on our way from school
to home? We raced to the tune
of bicycles along three trails
named after the Marx Brothers,
bendy trails on a landfill
full of scavenging, quarrel-
some birds and smells, so
funky, brewing in a giant
cauldron under our bicycles,
nostril-stinging vapours that we
called the armpit of the world,
our city, au naturel with patchy
grass for chin stubble, boulders
for teeth dodged by our wheels.

2.
Speed-bumped, pot-holed streets
twist axles, extract exhaust pipes,
idle hands pull off tree limbs,
insect wings, roots, but no past
in hot house blues, rock, no roll,
drop dead and bury where you
drop, nameless, unmarked grave
body bound spine turning over
underground scanned by worms
hooked on birdsong, deep throat
hydraulics, sans politics, with body
parts in bits from the other half
wanted but no reward for a bark
for an overbite, for rocks so bright
their music jumps off cliffs onto

solid rocks where dolphins slide
by without a peep no current,
drive, paddle or compass
for gold in the mouth, cap twist
on hat, sideburns crisp as bones
through a flat nose, hole in ears
for diamonds with blood on them
father before proper man form
in your head, first shot from thigh
not low and too high to count,
how many trees knocked down for this,
how many birds lose feathers,
eggs smashed in nests for this,
trees torn by machines operated
round the clock by helmets
on clown faces painted red
on double time and no fault
no crime, says the man suit
on the remote, behind security,
for the price of my skin is sin
and the hair on my head falls
out for a cause on a frontline
with a dolphin smile and pink
slip economy, read about this
in Deuteronomy, prehistory
christens me for post-doctoral
histories of slave ship decrees

3.
After the relegation game, fans
broke bottles and marched
along the entirety of Compton
Avenue on the roofs, bonnets and
trunks of cars, walking on air,
singing 'You'll never walk alone'.
They pulled up young trees
planted by the Council and used
the support staves as javelins.
The police herded them into vans.
Pubs served as sanctuaries for some.

A postman lost his front teeth
and turban and the day's mail
flew away like kites cut from
their strings, there was one shoe
with a slant wear in the heel
belonging to one bare foot some-
where in the city, but this shoe,
picked up by a street-sweeper,
kicks about between three hills
Groucho, Harpo and Chico
no top hat, monocle or coat-tails.
Try on this shoe, tap your way
out, or be consumed by this place.

The Rose of Toulouse

1.
If it exists, smells of buttered croissants,
Strawberry jam and café au lait.

The anti-terrorist knife just about splits
Crumbly, boomerang-shaped bread and sends
Legions marching to Paris in Roman formation

Patterns of the dominated, with a streetwise hip
And nightclub hop and not a slave to be seen,
And certainly not a scene for former slaves

Or their feisty descendants, wearing their life
Savings, nursing wounds from history, no track
Record in an ocean with bones for a library.

2.
This is my last morning in this town,
But not the last town I will see this morning.

I head for the capital where the talk
Is less sonorous as sonorous goes,
Tongues less forked, more clipped,

With the colonial emblems of slaves on the streets
Looking proprietorial in their Nike fatigues,
My brothers and sisters in arms, in the daily

Grind to keep that grin and in-your-face,
Game-face from turning sour, keep dancing
For suppers and Lucky Strikes.

3.
I love this time to myself and miss my kids
Climbing all over my writing routine pretence,

When I want nothing to do with them
And want nothing to do with anything
That does not include them in it.

My dreams do not count, too many to count,
I recount the majority as nightmares.
Please do not give me what I ask for.

I do not know what I want;
I do not want what I know.
I am in at least two minds about this,

4.
That and *de tarat* as Guyanese say
Waving away confusion morphed into

Pesky houseflies craving salt on a brow.
There is a word for my condition,
But I won't find it and cure myself.

There is a condition for my words
Spread slap-dash method on a palette
Governed by mood, governed in turn

By shape-shift focus as if that imagined
Rose of Toulouse with a city mix of sweets,
Grime and sirens, could ever be real.

5.
For this shared bread, for the multitudes
Housed in cardboard shelters on artificial hills

Of a city's fuming rubbish, and for my children
Whose gleeful faces rise in bubbles containing
Sky and everything underneath, as they sail

From me seeking death's light touch,
More a soundless kiss of dissolution
Of earth, sky and everything in between, I say,

We were people before we were slaves, pirates,
Or prostitutes with looks and matching smell.

Saturday, Ocean Creek

Sometimes the morning shakes itself from its moorings
To this world and lifts skywards with a fighter jet's roar,
Everyone lucky enough to be up and about looks to the east

But the sound follows idly a much faster comet too quick
For lazy eyes, so we ink in a sleek cross with exhausts
And settle for sound in place of sight for peace of mind.

A morning without wings, or adrift on one wing-beat,
Skimming waves for their fumes and salt-lick
That's gulls, waves, and wind, sharpening pines.

That's me happy to see that I am nowhere to be found,
Thrilled to be lost at last in things outside of myself
Until I belong to a world that ignores my footprint:

That pine umbrella, a flock, a handclap away from lift-off;
The pike of a heron, on one pirate-foot, stalking its reflection.

Calypso History Lesson

Son, kick off your shoes and come back with me
To what some call bush, what I know as country.
Where land fenced by thick forest and deep sea
And each day starts without the curse of history.

History cannot get a grip in that unfettered place,
The history you wake up with, just rinse your face.
History binds your sleep, straps a clock around your waist.
Penitence to history is our people's biggest waste.

The luck of youth is the joy to start from scratch,
Just find the burden of history, strike a match
And move on in a merry jaunt, not a frog-march,
Shirt-neck fling open, no tie and stiff starch.

History is a nation attached to your skin
For light to shine at and blind, not enlighten.
Unzip that fool's suit they say you born in,
That some fool zip on when you were sleeping.

Walk in the country, feel mud suck your toes,
Breathe, see how fresh air stings your city nose.
Take in the philosophy that nature's art shows
Without an invoice or price tag, without a boast.

I lost the same thing in this capital's streets
Of bare knuckles, spit, and bared teeth,
My body jacked by trainers on my feet,
History handcuffed me and shout, *thief.*

The country realigns your sorry backbone.
The country is the place your spine calls home.
You come to the country when you dead and gone,
Only then history content to leave you alone.

From American Vulture

The Vulture Goddess

In ancient Egypt she guards
tombs with talons of steel.

Her red apron of regurgitated
food for her young.

The couples look alike, exactly
alike, feathers hide everything.

The children all sound the same
in a playground of shrieks.

A carcass splayed out in the open
waits to be picked clean.

The line down the centre of a road
is white and red and full of flesh.

The birds rise up to avoid traffic
and drop back to feed in the wake.

They keep half an eye on the road
and half on target for beak and feet.

Think of them as operators
of a laundromat where every item

gradually disappears to leave
clean space robbed of bad smells.

Think how our path would be
if we had to wait on the slower work

of worms, deaf and without nostrils,
indifferent to us, some taped in us,

until we fall in their blind path,
and thank these gods in our midst.

Vulture Highway Code

What's in the road
stays in the road

When the broken white lines are joined by red
pay close attention

Indicate with a tip of the wing when swooping up
or down or turning left or right

One wingbeat lets a bird ride for miles
in magazine fashion

The road not taken has no carrion
and is not worth a second look

Eating on the road requires a bird's full attention
positively no multi-tasking

The engine coming up your rear is the engine
you need to fear

The dot in the distance that grows larger by the second wants a
                                               reaction from you
react or do not at your peril

What is behind the wheel will one day be in front
what is in front was once behind

Spare a feather for the poor bird that mistook a windscreen for
                                                     a mirror
and stared into it (or should that be steered)

Though we are the colour of the road
we must never colour the road

The white lines down the middle are the bands borrowed
from around our necks

The hard shoulder bears no relation to the cold shoulder
though both are hard and neither belongs to us

We are birds first and roadsters second
this is not a chicken and egg situation

Your only gamble should be never to end up flat
as a playing card in the road

Vulture Red Letter Day

Vulture days when she feels there's no wet in the rain
When no two wingbeats sound alike

On such days she should just chill on a ledge and watch worlds fly by,
But no, she be vulture and she won't let nothing go nowhere,
Not without her say so.

In her mood she pushes from her perch into a breeze full of
                                                    sweet things.

The moment she leaps she knows she made a big mistake
But one thing leads to another and other things take over

Before she knows it she's in the thick of a carcass set upon
By a crew drawn from miles around by a smell as rich as any seam,
Crack, crevice, fold, mould, groove.

She pins flesh with feet, lowers head, fails to hear the engine approach.

Vulture's Theory of Perpetual Return

I fly up and float on one wingbeat for as long as I can make circles
in the circling winds, I see the same things all the time and all that
time
I see those same things differently.

The maze in the trees keeps me counting the trees in the maze.
Something in my gut tells me I am not what I eat, but what
I eat tells me not to believe everything my stomach tells me.

The meat I ingest, in all seriousness, is the meat I regurgitate.
The call I launch into the wind is a boomerang.
My shadow rides the plains below and thinks its shadow rides the
winds.

My feather loosens like a human tooth in a human dead head.
I must be human too, destined for a hole in the ground if lucky,
luckier still, to grace a table for vultures known as the most
enthusiastic of eaters.

The lamplighter who lights all the lamps above
lights the lamps of my eyes and how that lamplighter douses
those cold flames so too my eyes turn dark.

I belong to no one and no one wants me when I am gone,
to where I do not know, except for the sound just before
silence and the silence just after sound.

Vulture in El Dorado

Of the mind
Of unruffled feathers

Of bird above bushy cloud in space flight
Of breeze flying me

Of my shadow racing under beside ahead behind and yes on top me
Of my beak fast asleep on a pillow filled with meat

Of nightmare vegetables dive-bombing me
Of the guy in Guyana and his Ana and me

Of the venison in Venezuela
Of the pepper in Cayenne

Of the felled feathers of trees floating down the Demerara and
                                                        Essequibo
Of my hollow bones all ready to be a flute

Of my beak for the end of a spear
Of my claws stringed for a warrior-necklace

Of the gold pieces in my stomach that help break down my food
Of my high up lookout look down on this live theatre-in-the-round

Of my wishes granted every day to sniff out the dead uprights
Of my rocket-climb in my sleep up up up to greet my stop-time

Emily Dickinson, How Does Your Garden Grow?

for Julian May, Sarah Hemming, Seamus, Gabriel and Matthew

1.

I navigate roads cut through hills
decorated fall, New England style.

Each bend slides off my windscreen,
turns a fresh page wild with paint.

Things move so fast they evade
their names and when I fix them under

my photosensitive dark, bifocal gaze,
they run like newsprint in the rain.

What a palette! A season spread on
tectonic plates, a scrubbed sky rinses,

brushes and loads boughs of colours
with arrows of light, sky that refills

for more brush dips, more flurries,
re-plaster, distress, veined leaf,

limbs, trunks and mercurial roads.
Five states later I face Main Road,

Amherst, Massachusetts, and a train,
stanzas adrift in iambs, shouldering

hills stacked in rows whose shelves
tenured librarians tidy for more leaves,

more borrowings by hook and crook,
squirrel, deer, and crows reviewing things

from above, caw–caw close to ridicule,
love vilified for a return to the same site

where trauma, in white gown and gloves,
wears a mask, in studio lights, and waits.

In walks Emily, her several lives,
mark floors, her scanning them, over

years, so boardwalks and kickboards
talk her kept memory – so I fancy,

her gait, shuffle, swing and groove;
worn stairs, impressed by her weight,

over years that amount to art in her life,
in a life of art. Where she stopped I hope

to start; where Copland leads, I follow
coupled to her engine and his tracks.

2.

Her four walls sport a neutral off-white,
a few wall hangings, no-nonsense look
to the place, a handful of steps from one
wall to the next, four windows for flight.

Her desk, pushed close to a wall and closer
to the heater and angled to see out but not
be seen while looking, furthest from door,
remembers her lean into it if nothing else.

Imagine a field across Main Street
banked by hedgerows and bordered
by hills she knows keep their distance
but feels she might reach out and touch.

That desk keeps her chained all day
except for meals, occasional bathroom

breaks, and an impulse to push away
from it and run for her life beyond

garden gate and picket fence for street
after unpaved street until she bumps
into those hills and climbs that blue
beyond her conviction honed in her garden.

But street is another country not sought
nor found and therefore never to be won or
even lost. Other people remain ghosts
crossing Main Street noisily, voices,

footfall, clatter. She lives by jumping
from her time, from her place to mine,
other worlds found in tea leaves,
biscuit crumbs, every morsel a universe,

each patterned spread of strained tea
a history with her, not many people,
her desk, this room, whose walls melt
before my disbelieving prescription lens.

3.

Skull for a room, room with a view,
walls have ears, air tunnels through.
Eyes look in, as much as out,
this room talks with a kissing mouth.

Skull fitted to flesh and laced bones,
hard walls around vaulted marrow,
balanced on a fulcrum of stones,
driven by a river under the skin.

This is thought on a flicked flint,
sparks fly as Emily Dickinson thinks
for sun to drive away chiselled rain,
for a lover without a proper name.

4.

Emily in her garden neat as a book
lined with petals pressed between leaves
sewn together by her hand and labelled
with the stuff that runs in her veins.

Emily in her room where she paces
lengthy roots of a tree, she carves
routes as many as that tree with its head
adrift in cloud and thick hair spread

underground so that limbs in air match
roots in soil with earth surface as mirror,
trunk leans, stares into, as much as cranes
and peers at blue, neither one more true;

both promise that tree seasons and rings
on each finger to measure the years
it takes to make a garden worth of books
and a book for each season in a garden.

5.

More than once Emily holds out her hair
to light and thinks each strand
carries life she might lead in another
setting. For a while she collects
her hair from comb and brush to stop

crows spiriting away bundles
to feather a nest. She tries
not to count the grey hairs
beginning to multiply and wins
enough time to count the few black hairs

feathering her skull. She feels
her bones freed of muscle and sinew.
Ice in her veins starts to freeze.
She tries her best to enjoy the view.

6.

I drive from Main Street and cannot look
up at the rearview, not with its glass melting
until it resembles a circus mirror I stand

before and do not know whether to laugh
or run from that place for somewhere less
revealing, so I drive and pray for green

lights all the way out of Amherst, for if I stop
I fear I might be forced to turn around,
force another return to look at a glass

half full with my image from a past beyond
my grasp, when stamps on an envelope
seemed negligible for the price and paper

cuts healed with a lick of my spit, so that I saw
what cannot be seen or felt, what once was.

7.

Yesterday a hummingbird parted air
before my face and I mistook it for a bumblebee
and fled, but it waited for me to look again,
see for a second time, and my first up-close

look, a rapid pulse wrapped in feathers,
trying to unravel the bundle of itself without success.
I inched forward but it zipped away and left me
fronting an absence for what had been my past.

On the wrong side of fifty, I wish to slow
what time's left to count those wing-beats,
stretch what remains, with me, not in a daze.
Come back bee lookalike, part the air again,

I promise to hold my breath and stay rooted,
us, so near, I see two of me in one of you.

The Storm

Was I always like this, a watcher first and a doer second?
Twenty children ran from the house to greet the storm.

But not me. I stayed on the porch and studied them.
They cartwheeled as lightning rolled dice overhead.

Something crawled under my skin for me to join them;
An impulse that I had to fight to keep in check.

I looked at the nearest grownup to make doubly sure
It was all right and saw no reaction, just watchfulness,

A peer up at the blackness thickening and a glance at us,
And not much more than a pulling close of an open shirt.

And so I dived off the front porch and into field grass
With the others and pitched defiance (gobbled up by

The hungry wind throwing its weight around)
At the strapping dark, whistling trees, pushing them

This way and that for fun, with twigs and leaves torn
And flung in our faces and water lashed at us.

As lightning squared up directly overhead, white sheets
Cast wide and deep with us for fish to gather up,

Aunts and uncles called us in, and the stragglers by name.
We filled all the windows for the rest of the show.

We were loud, jittery, spastic, giddy, and at one
With the storm whose current ran in us and made us

Beg to go back out in the open, to throw up our arms
For the wind and the lightning to claim us all

As their offspring and drag us up into their embrace,
Beyond the reach of adults calling, calling our names.

The Fence

Whose translated missing paling
I duck through to exit the front yard
For a field where an alligator spent
An afternoon lassoed to a fence post
And we stoned, prodded and shouted at it
To chase us thinking we'd run in a zigzag
To safety, that paling like a missing tooth
Remembered by a searching tongue,
That untranslatable paling.

Back again as never before
With a gap my head cannot slip through.
Call it loose rather than missing,
Easy to swing to one side for a sideways
Duck through a gap made for children.
My head is much the same size;
The fence changed its mind
About me as someone fit to slip
Through it without a second thought.

Why should this concern the field?
It absorbed that alligator and covered
The spot where the alligator lay
With print-erasing grass which I pull
In long strands and throw as far
As I can only to have the strands
Fly back into my face like spit
Launched against a strong breeze:
Paling, first missing, next loose, now gone.

Night Swim

I remove my eyes,
My rayon skin,
My spare-tyre feet
And dive into my reflection

Braced for a collision.

The earth opens as if dug
Just for me, a reservation
I made well in advance,
Expecting this day would
Creep up on me.

Water wide with my ripples,
With a hummingbird's
Accuracy for each pore
On my body, keep me like you:
Buoyant, pliable and true.

The Giant of Land's End

The giant of Land's End
Lives far from our town
Where the river bends
Towards barren down.

He shuns consensus
Malls and traffic jams,
Dodges the city census,
TV and dotcom scams.

His peat and thatch house
Crouches on a hillside,
Like a foxhole or dugout
Hidden from prying eyes.

His front door faces the sea,
His backdoor kisses the banks
Of a twisting, warbling estuary,
Where he fishes and thinks.

When he's far from home
It's to hunt wild game
He clobbers with a stone
If they keep still when he aims.

But he catches only what
He can eat and eats only
What he needs to live so that
Everything he touches solely

For life understands him,
Including trout hooked on
The end of a fishing line,
Held by him in his reflection:

A face of bunched features,
Big nose and fat lips,
Hair of a wild creature,
Broad shoulders, broad hips.

How our paths crossed
When I least expected
When all I'd heard said
He never existed,

I cannot explain,
I know he never wanted
Me to experience his pain
Or to leave me haunted.

I skip town with my spars
For a day in the country,
For some R and R far
From our town's hurly-burly

That gets little done,
After a lot of plenty
Put in by everyone
Running on empty.

We drive till roads
Turn into tracks,
We park and unload
The SUV's roof-rack.

Next we walk single
File and laugh till we hurt
At our bursts of jingles
From famous adverts

Stop for lunch by a bog
Beside a stream and drink
All the brews we lugged
This far, and give thanks

To Bacchus, for his smarts
About fermenting grapes,
To the country for its art
Putting up us town-types;

Pick a tree each to piss
Against and the same wind
To whistle into as we piss,
Wind whispering leaf and limb.

We're tipsy, otherwise
We would not have done
What we do next, as unwise
As any drunk decision:

We decide to split up, go solo
For a while with the country,
For the quiet and rococo
Of our own company.

(Big mistake some say,
What were you guys thinking?
We weren't. We were at play,
Our sole guide was instinct.)

There seems no harm
In it, and with cellphones,
Not hard to keep within arm's
Length of a safe zone.

We draw straws for a pole.
I pick South, the shortest
Straw, Woody, North, Nicole,
East, that leaves Rick with West.

I decide to walk for a few
Minutes in one direction,
Then turn left, and do
More time, no option

But that left turn until
I end up where I started,
By that bog and its landfill
Smell as if we'd all farted.

Where I expect to meet
Most if not all of my crew,
Grinding their bored teeth
And craving another brew.

I hear a groan and grunt,
Not soft from injury
But exasperated, blunt,
I look but can't see

Beyond the screen of wood
So walk towards what I know
Has to be the moaner Woody,
And try to guess what now.

I pick up water's allure,
Figure Woody's wet more
Than he wanted, therefore
Mad with the stream, sore

From walking these woods,
Until I part the twigs
With a few choice words
For him and freeze in mid-

Sentence: there, in front
My eyes, by the creek,
Is a thing big as an elephant,
A man whose bulk I see

More as a beast's than one
Of us, a thing you go to the top
Of a beanstalk to stumble upon;
So otherworldly, you throw up

When you clap eyes on him,
So that I gasp and stagger,
While he, about to swim,
Breaks from his stupor,

Whips his boulder-head
Around and locks my gaze,
Appears to mouth *You're dead*
As he pushes his supersize

Onto two tree-trunk legs
To give chase. I turn and split,
Hear branches snap, as if pegs
Hung them in place or spit

As he parts them to catch
Me, which he does in nano-
Seconds since I cannot match
His two steps for my nine.

He picks me up, off my legs,
By my backpack, with one hand.
I bicycle-kick and doggie-paddle
Floating at my height over land.

Don't hurt me, don't hurt me!
I scream at his bellybutton,
And in the less than three
Seconds he keeps me airborne,

It dawns he hasn't the first
Notion what to do: beat, eat, and/
Or treat me as compost.
My OfficeMax manager DNA

Takes over, I order the giant
To put me down this instant,
Or else; or else what, I haven't
The foggiest. He obeys, I think

More from surprise at an order
From me, his plaything, than
Any gene-wiring to take orders
From a body less than

Half his size. He floors
Me, or I fall, more like flail
Inelegantly, onto all fours,
When my backpack strap fails.

I scramble up and swivel
Face-to-face with him,
My arms at pugilist level,
But drop them like pins

When I see what stands six
Feet opposite me: an obelisk
Made of concrete and brick,
With battering rams for fists.

The forest tilts like scenery
Hung wrong, next a white
Flash paints all the greenery
White, finally, instant night.

Call it a man fainting or call
Me a swooning lady at court,
When a wit's gaze falls
On me I hit cold earth.

Legs like jelly, eyes rolled
Back in my Google-filled head.
That's me in my jungle-role
Of terror, that's my street-cred

Gone south, the way of all
Bravura after the bars close
And we reduce to a foetal
Position hugging a pillow.

The best and the worst of men
Asleep for a third of our almanac.
He must have scooped me
Up and carried me back

To his place. My next sight
Is his musty, damp and drab
Hovel with no natural light.
I bolt upright and grab

Onto a high-backed chair,
The size of a throne,
To steady my legs and clear
My head and find I am alone.

This is my one chance
To look around, but I fly
For the front entrance
And grab my phone and try

Speed-dialling a friend,
But no signal, no bars,
No stripes, no satellite
To bounce off, no stars.

Just a giant I meet
At the door, lenses
Glazed waiting for me
To come to my senses.

He does little to stop
Me in my tracks.
I sit by him in a squat
Like his with my back

Slightly curved like his
And my arms on my knees
And my hands open, not fists
In a move to put him at ease.

People will come looking
For me, you know mate.
I know. When you took
Me here you made a mistake.

Maybe. He understands
Me and he talks as well.
I get a book-deal, news-stands
Full-of-us, talk-shows smell.

Some of which he sniffs
And does not like the whiff
Of not one little bit
But we stay in our mirror sitting

Position to see if trust
Might with luck break out,
Despite it all, between us,
Since trust takes two.

I do not see my friends
Gather with my backpack
Which one of them finds
With its telltale broken strap.

I don't hear their panic
About my likely fate
I imagine they feel sick
With guilt as freight,

Since it was me not them
Who was missing, and me
Not them who might be
Dead meat, lost, or hemmed

In somewhere dark
And damp with insects
That creep and spark
And bite off your sex.

That would be balls
In another context
Not these hallowed halls
Of poetry and text

Garnished for academic
Consumption with a cherry
Of narrative that's pandemic
Right now in every

Published story or poem.
None of this would make
Sense to the giant, some
Say, but he could tell fake

From real, and truth
From poetry and fiction.
And which of these brutes
Does he think I come from?

We sit facing each
Other by the stream
I listen to water and watch
Him without seeming

To, that is, out of
The corner of my eyes
By staring just above
Where my hook lies

In slow-rolling water,
Element I worship,
My sign and alma mater,
Working its scholarship

On me in ways I cannot
See but know after
The fact, whose tonic
Laces my laughter.

For this he seizes
A huge flat stone,
And this I want to see,
How he gets it done.

He walks as I trot
To keep up, the great lump
Comes to a sudden stop,
Acts like a tree stump.

What a ticket,
I marvel, a few feet
Away in a thicket,
Where I count pleats

In bark so old it peels
Like a sunburn,
Bark older than sleep,
Back-dated by carbon.

Sure enough a deer
Ambles along and starts
Nosing around near
The Henry Moore art

Exhibit left in the wild
For natural consumption:
A giant man with a child's
Hunting assumption

That all things come
To him who waits,
Including wholesome
Game in a deer's shape.

Now the deer is still,
Stone in his hand,
Swing and crush skull
In one swift blow and

Do not make it soft,
Do not take too long,
Swing hard for that life's
Interrupted song.

Why wait, Mr Overgrown?
Strike the damn thing.
Swing the blasted stone.
Deer must be tired grazing,

That must be the reason
He lowers his crude
Choice of a weapon
In slow motion and the food

Bolts into my bush
And knocks me flying
As if that giant crushed
My skull without trying.

I do not say a word.
He can read my face.
We trudge back mad
At this unforgiving place.

He showed me his true
Hand, among those trees
He froze as our meal flew,
Leaving us a diet of berries.

He let me eat first:
A handful of worms
That wriggled; the worst
I could do was squirm

At grub from the root of palms.
The stream to wash it down.
At last he says in a calm
Voice, Go back to your town.

I do not linger to hear
Him a second time.
I just run from there
And stop at a forest sign

That bans hunting
And find men out looking
For me and tell them nothing
Worth putting in a book.

The media would make
Mincemeat of him.
The authorities would break
His spirit in their museum.

I asked him about family,
Where he came from,
How he lived so minimally
Not dependent on anyone

But himself without feeling
Miserable and lonely.
He was born concealing
Himself he says, an only

Child on a sheep farm.
It was easy to grow
Fast and escape the harm
Of teasing and aggro

From peers and gossip
Common in villages.
He could see traffic
Approach his farm ages

Before it got there,
So had plenty of time
To hide and let his dear
Parents deal with them.

One day both died
(He found them in bed)
From carbon monoxide
Poisoning, so he fled,

After a two-day vigil
In their bedroom
Hoping they might still
Be alive but in a coma.

He wants to be left
Alone with his grief.
Keep our meeting to yourself.
I swear on my mother's life.

I send him positive vibes
Daily, as the brother
I found and lost and tried
Finding out about before

Losing him to that place.
We share a black skin
In a mean time of race
Wars, that makes us kin.

I said to him, 'But you
Mouthed *You're dead*
To me, that's why I flew.'
'No, I said *You're Fred*.

I know you because mum
Had you adopted weeks
After you were born,
Fearing another freak

Of nature as I was called
By midwife and doctors.
My folks hid me from all
Prying eyes and malefactors.

It meant I lost a brother
And won this private life.'
Either I bring a city's bother
To him, or I lose him twice.